Power Play

Power Play

Get a job NOW

- Skip past conventional search methods
- Vastly *increase* your chances of success
- Vastly *decrease* the time spent on your job search

Mark P. Williamson,
Executive Recruiter

Copyright © 2012, Mark P. Williamson

All rights reserved. No part of this book may be reproduced, stored, or transmitted by any means—whether auditory, graphic, mechanical, or electronic—without written permission of both publisher and author, except in the case of brief excerpts used in critical articles and reviews. Unauthorized reproduction of any part of this work is illegal and is punishable by law.

ISBN 978-1-300-09268-1

Table of Contents

Part 1: Intersection of Interests, Ability, and Marketability 1
    The "Advice" Letter 5
    Zigs and Zags 7
    Who Benefits from Applying the Advice of This Guide? 17
    Best Intentions Conventions 18
    Reality Check 24

Part 2: Gaming Your Odds 27
    Get Motivated, Yes! 30
    Methodology 31

Part 3: The Pitch 33
    Practice and Hone Your Script 38
    Sample Pitches 40

Part 4: The Call List 45
    Manage the Process 48
    Making the Calls 49
    Why Not the HR Department: The Case Against 62

Part 5: You Be the Judge 69
    Notes on Conventional Sources of Help 69
    Surely, These Folks Can Help 73
    What's Missing? 75

Conclusions 77

Part 1
Intersection of Interests, Ability, and Marketability

Careers can be tricky business. Much of what we accomplish in our careers depends on our abilities, and yet a good deal of career success depends on the interests that drive us. Some people are fortunate enough to recognize their own inherent *abilities*. Others are fortunate to have strong career *interests*. Ultimately, each group must somehow find *economic marketability*. There is a rare group that is blessed to have their interests match up with their abilities. Rarer still is the group whose *strong interest* matches their *strong abilities*; together they have real *economic marketability*. Many lawyers, investment bankers, and entrepreneurs are prevalent to this group. Such individuals thrive and prosper, often remaining on a single path that leads to progressively higher levels of responsibility and financial reward.

Then there are the rest of us: the great majority of job- and career-seekers, the great majority who follow a decidedly less direct path. Consider *yourself* for a minute as you ponder these three variables: interest, ability, and marketability. What are your interests? What are your abilities? What is your real value to any company?

I am not asking what it is you think you can do. Given the fact *you will face direct competition from others for career opportunities*, I am asking for an honest assessment of your value to a prospective company.

Why you, and not someone else?

This self-assessment of work place value can be seen as a constant. As you review this book, keep in mind there are many zigzags you cannot control that can affect career prospects. These include:

- The economy
- One's own interests
- Personal situations
- State and federal governmental policies
- Technology
- The status of one's specific industry
- Cultural tastes and cultural evolution

These variables affect job opportunities in unpredictable ways. Little can be done about this unpredictability, it's just the way of the world: you might have an ill family member to attend to, you may be the last remaining COBOL software programmer, you might be a mortgage broker affected by the many governmental rule changes after the fallout of the 2008 subprime meltdown, your marketing efforts may be largely connected to print media. These are all examples of the unpredictability and how your career prospects can quickly change.

On the other hand, there's something else that's unpredictable: the opportunities that exist only in the minds of hiring managers. At any given moment, hiring managers have, among their many responsibilities, staffing needs to be addressed, i.e. a person or persons must be hired. Hiring managers may or may not have communicated these needs with their company, but in all cases, they are ripe for a conversation as to what is needed and in what timeframe. Though seemingly random, erratic, and, arbitrary, these opportunities can be discovered and harvested by you, the job seeker.

As a professional recruiter, I have received hundreds of résumés from those that I knew were wasting their time contacting me and would ultimately meet with great difficulty in their search for a job.

President of the "Waiting for His Ship to Come In" Club

I have witnessed mistake after mistake, misdirected efforts, and time wasted—all in which no job was secured. Not a surprising result to me, because, in my experience, most job search methods include quite a bit of *self-delusion*—the hope that conventional job search efforts will yield results, even those these efforts are highly unlikely to come in contact with the staffing needs dancing in the heads of hiring managers.

In any event, from these thousands of observations, I amassed insights and strategies that I learned could be infinitely better and more effective, strategies independent of a person's situation or background. That last part was not a small thing, so let's repeat it: strategies *independent* of a person's current situation or background, meaning this guide will demonstrate how you can succeed in a job search despite your background or circumstance. Whenever I could, I'd send an email containing advice on how he or she could help him/herself. Over time, the advice page was refined and enhanced. That advice is now the framework of this guide.

The advice seeks to make clear to a jobseeker how he or she can:

1) **Increase** the odds of getting a job
2) **Decrease** the time it takes to get a job

The "Advice" Letter

"Dear _____,
Here is my advice on how you can help yourself with your own job search:

- Get a list of fifty to a hundred companies you want to work for (easy to obtain).
- Find the names of two or three decision makers at each company (examples are VPs of operations, VPs of engineering, directors of marketing, logistics managers, etc). You can get the names via websites, industry directories, or by simply calling the company and asking the receptionist.

- *DO NOT BOTHER to email, fax, or submit your résumé through a website; such activities are largely a waste of your time and only serve to discourage a person.*
- Instead, spend all your time directly speaking to decision makers by calling them on the phone. Follow this guide:

    1) Prepare in writing what you will say. This will be your script.
    2) Have your script ready.
    3) Practice saying your script aloud a few times.
    4) Be prepared to tell the decision maker: who you are, what makes you distinctive, the particular value you can deliver, what exactly it is you want. Be specific: refer to job functions and job titles. Ask if they have a current need for someone of your skills and abilities.
    5) Make the calls to each and every decision maker, *one right after the other.*
    6) *Keep track of whom you spoke to, take notes of everything that was said.*
    7) Follow up as necessary with second and third calls until you have a conversation with each

decision maker, in the quest to discover who has a need of your services.

You will have the job you seek shortly, as a direct result of these calls. *And* you will have established contact with an incredible group of industry decision makers, some who will have an interest in you in the future!

Now, take a deep breath. Good luck!

Mark Williamson, Executive Recruiter

In sections ahead, for each and every element of the above, we will be drilling down to subterranean levels to show step-by-step how anyone can game the odds in his or her favor. Hang in there.

Zigs and Zags

After having spent my freshman year studying liberal arts at Dickinson College in Carlisle, Pennsylvania, I received a finance degree from the University of Oklahoma in May 1984. After an initial six-month stint in Washington, DC working the retail counter of an old Deak-Perera foreign exchange office, I eventually landed a position as a financial analyst in the finance department of EDS (Electronic Data Systems), the company formed by former presidential candidate, H. Ross Perot.

Landing this role took about *eight months* of concerted effort using *inferior techniques that will be identified later in this guide as categorically ineffective. Look at the time these techniques took to work: eight months!* After a few frustrating years at EDS, aptitude testing revealed the source of the frustration: I have no inherent aptitude for abstract visualization (the aptitude required to process abstract concepts quickly, such as finance and accounting), but it was discovered I have strong aptitudes for certain engineering disciplines such as mechanical, civil, structural, petroleum, and biomedical, as well as strong aptitudes for conductive and deductive reasoning. The testing eventually led to my receiving a bachelor's degree in mechanical engineering from the University of Texas at Austin in August 1991.

Admittedly, the fall of 1991 saw a mild recession, but the job search still took four, long depressing months. And, since each month back then was worth $3,000 per month in salary, a search method capable of trimming even a single month from the search would result in an additional $3,000 in my pocket, pretty basic math. (We will come back to this.)

The methods I used to secure my next role actually contained small glimpses of the techniques you will be using when following this guide. The successful application of these steps landed me in Houston, Texas in May 1992, employed with an industrial elevator manufacturer. However, after working there in a hybrid commercial-technical role, something still seemed unaddressed for me, career-wise.

After a couple of years with the elevator manufacturer, I came to understand just how much my boss (a guy who made it through maybe three semesters of college) had really accomplished by building a company that sells and rents construction elevators. I departed the company to give entrepreneurship a try (aptitude testing also revealed I should be my own boss, generally speaking), leading eventually to the marketing and selling of US-made sporting goods to Hungarian wholesalers from a base in Budapest, Hungary. *Yes, really.*

Still, my preparation to direct and grow my own business seemed thin, so in 1995, I returned to academia one last time, this time to Rice University in Houston, where I received an MBA in 1997. After a couple more entrepreneurial ventures, one involving the production and marketing of Securities and Exchange Commission training videos covering the fundamentals of US Securities law (*still not kidding*), I eventually accepted a role as VP of business development for a Chinese-based "dot-com" called Intermost Corporation. I relocated to Mainland China in the city of Shenzhen where I remained until well after the dot-com/stock market meltdown of both Intermost and the entire "dot-com" phenomenon in March 2000.

After leaving the collapsed Chinese firm came the real career curveball. During the 2001–2002 recession that followed the stock market collapse, I decided to take a shot at professional stone sculpting *(again, no joke)*. (I did actually have a history of so-called artistic talent, identified by schoolteachers all the way back in kindergarten.) I decided to combine marketing and strategy principles (and, yes, even some engineering principles) in the creation of bronze, marble, porcelain, and granite sculpture. I relocated a bit during this time: Manhattan, Santa Fe, Europe, and then back to Texas. I aggressively pursued sculpture as a profession for six years, securing representation in a few galleries, attending a plethora of chardonnay-and-cheese art openings, obtaining press and news coverage, and sometimes sales and commissions.

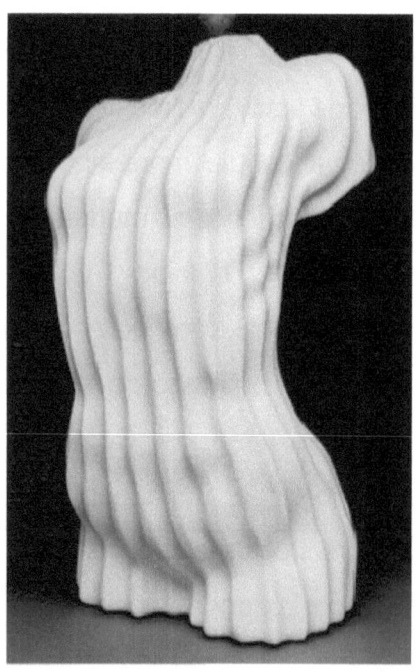

"Lila," Mark Williamson, 2002

Do you remember the three important variables for career success I mentioned?

1) Ability
2) Interest
3) Marketability

At the end of the day, I concluded that, although *able* to produce sculpture on a professional level and having an *interest* in doing so, the *marketability* was not enough to keep a dieting sparrow alive. I had to move on.

By summer of 2008, my own financial situation dictated the need to pull together all of the career variables, get focused, and leverage these experiences and degrees into a financially viable career opportunity. *Imagine what my résumé looked like by 2008.* Not exactly the most marketable résumé:

- All over the map
- Different industries
- No company loyalty in sight
- Flakey-looking (make that *really* flakey-looking)
- Unrelated professions

What company in the entire US would consider hiring me? I had to think of other avenues, mostly business ideas that I could quickly make viable that would not require a company to hire me. *My only path to career success was to hire myself.*

Let's step back for a moment, and consider the *natural consequences* that flowed from my career decisions, effectively closing off certain options. For example, I could have sucked it up, kept my head down, and toughed it out at EDS (a company now unrecognizable from the 1980s, its remnants now part of HP). As an almost philosophical point, I would have locked myself in an environment in which I could not effectively compete, one in which I had no real interest (*one of the required career success variables*). Lack of fairness in life aside, this guide directs attention **away** from uncontrollable variables (such as "fairness") and delivers actions you **can** control.

In July 2008, I drove to Colorado to deliver and install my final commissioned work, a 2500-pound granite sculpture, my sculpting swansong. On August 3, 2008, I signed on the dotted line, purchased a recruiting franchise, and began recruiting engineers for the oil and gas industry.

Mark P. Williamson

"Sloan," Mark Williamson, 2004

"Transparent Ego," Mark Williamson, 2006

Ever since then, I have observed, day in and day out at a professional level, what works and what does not when it comes to job search activities and what it takes to actually secure a job. Many of the engineers and geoscientists I deal with have special and highly desirable skillsets and experiences, making them quite marketable. *But what about the great majority of careerists, who are good but not indispensable?*

Here is what I notice on a daily basis: **too many jobseekers tend to depend on others to find them a job**. Let's drill down this statement. Many of us have heard that securing a new job will be "the hardest job we ever face." There are good reasons this is so. It appears that no one but no one has created a generic process that is both easily understood and provides favorable results.

In the heady days of a job search, with your own welfare on the line (and perhaps also the welfare of other dependents), we demand results *and* speed. Obtaining only one or the other **stinks**. Speed can only solve the immediate problem of having no income or having no place to go every day, but speed alone can actually do more damage than good in the long run, i.e. being in a role that's not part of your future or career objectives. On the other hand, obtaining results (without speed) can mean watching months pass in order to finally land a meaningful and relevant job; this process can cost literally thousands of dollars with each passing month!

How can such an environment be allowed to continue in the face of the information age? There are two main reasons:

1) It is *human nature to avoid having to think*. We are in the friggin' Information Age of aps, devices, and instantaneity. We avoid having to figure it out, in this case, figuring out a fruitful job search process that can be followed and trusted to yield desired results. Rather than figure out a functional process, it is easier to depend on others, especially those *posing as so-called experts*. Look: you are knowledgeable in your area of focus, right? But that area of focus probably has nothing to do with a ready-to-go, mechanized job search. Surely, the experts have a handle on how to do that, right?

2) FYI: currently, there are plenty of companies and individuals on standby, claiming they can help you get a job. *Many times, they can!* But keep in mind, those that claim they will do the work for you are selling something; they have monetary reasons not to surrender control of this task. There are winners and losers in any endeavor in life, and a job search is no exception. Because groups that are selling something will *claim* they can help, these groups by default are also highly motivated to create an industry that purports it will help you find a new job. This industry is slick, formidable, and includes firms

that ask seductive questions like *"How much income do you want to make?"* furthering the illusion they are the answer to your job search challenges. In many cases, *this group makes money as long as you continue to remain unemployed.* Such a program is quite different from the method you will be learning in the pages ahead, different primarily in the form of cost (they will need $3,000 to $10,000 to "help" you find a job.

Quick story: the first petroleum engineer I placed with an exploration and production company shared with me that he had paid such a firm $5,000 just three months before locating me. You read that right: at a time when this person was looking to *receive* income, the dubious "job assistance" firm had this person giving *them* five grand (I landed him a job paying $14,000/month shortly thereafter. I collected a nice fee *from the hiring company*).

As I said before, many times, these companies and individuals can actually get you a job. But remember, this guide is not about occasional success. It is all about vastly increasing the odds and vastly increasing the speed versus all other conventional job search methods. This guide delivers a methodical, mechanized process that you control.

Who benefits from applying the advice of this guide?

- Anyone seeking a job for any reason—whether you have been let go or your company has downsized. Samples of such a case include elimination of your entire division or even the entire company being sold, ending your position altogether
- New and recent college graduates, now wondering what all that hard work was all about.
- Jobseekers from the administrative support levels all the way through the department directors.
- Anyone having working experience that includes a healthy amount of trial-and-effort, i.e. different types of jobs or industries were sampled along the way, perhaps creating the impression that you don't know what you want.
- Anyone seeking to move from one industry into a new industry.
- Those looking to re-enter the working world after taking years off to raise a family.

As mentioned earlier, the ability to succeed using this method is ***independent*** of your background, experience, or work history to this point in time. Whatever your career objectives, whatever your work experiences, whatever your academic background, it ***does not matter***.

Best Intentions Conventions

The time and effort required of most all conventional career searches relies heavily on the efforts of others: recruiters, HR department personnel, company websites administrators, friends, family, schools, placement center personnel, and of course government minions (ha ha!) We will take a close look at each of these traditional methods a little later. Our method shifts most control *away* from these groups, placing control into your own hands regarding your job search.

Just think of all the time, money, and effort you have invested so far in your career. If you have a long work history, then perhaps you have years of trial-and-error investments under your belt. Or, if you possess a college degree, what did that cost you? Fifty thousand dollars? Two hundred and fifty thousand? Not to mention four or five years of your life, ***per degree***. Do you really want to place something as important as your career, from which you derive financial security, happiness, and even self-actualization, into the hands of others who have agendas different from yours? Why would any of us place trust in such groups, knowing that a powerful alternative existed?

This begs the question: where among all that time, college, heartache, and late nights at work were you taught a sure-fire, mechanized, strategic process to **get a job faster** and **get a job on-target to your objectives**? Probably never.

Why not?

Why is there no universally tried-and-true method for pursuing and securing a job?

How

can

this

be?

As a professional recruiter, this question is similar to the question: "Why do we need recruiters?" We need recruiters because:

1. For psychological (issues related to the self-confidence of jobseekers) reasons,
2. For cultural (certainly in the US, issues related to an entitlement mentality) reasons, and

3. Good recruiters have professional relationships with companies doing the hiring, and stay abreast of the specific needs of the hiring companies; for individuals who can fulfill these specific needs, recruiters with talent deliver tremendous value to both the contracting company and the individual.

In my own experiences engaging with thousands of jobseekers (as noted above), there appears to be an undertone of expectation that securing a job is someone else's job, not your job. *Wow!* Really? *Really?* Perhaps the notion that "It's your job to find me a job" made more sense before the onset of access to incredible technology and instant communication. But in the here-and-now, everything moves fast, and information flows freely. No one other than *you* can seriously be willing to make such an intense personal effort, an effort that must be built from the ground up, each and every time. *No one except **you** has the incentive to put forth the effort towards something so personally important to **you**.* And you can! If only you knew what to do **and** how to set your expectations accordingly (both are required).

Wrong Turns

Does the following sound familiar? Here's a list of typical, conventional job search activities:

- Submit a résumé through company website. On the plus side, this act makes you feel good and gives you a sense of immediate accomplishment. But the odds of this working, in general, are very long, maybe even 1000-to-1. Companies are looking for specific skills sets and experiences and can afford to slowly harvest perfect matches over time. *Thank you for playing!*

- Ask your personal network of family and friends. How many of your friends and family are the exact decision makers for hiring someone like you? Again, one hell of a long shot.

- Post your résumé on career and job search websites. Similar to submitting a résumé through a company website, posting your résumé on career and job search websites: a) has an immediate effect on your sense of accomplishment and b) provides long odds for success. Then there is the ongoing effect, should no results be forthcoming, the psychological beat-down. Remember, companies are trolling for perfect matches to their needs.

- Reply to want ads. Same as online posting, *but slower.*

- Send résumé to recruiters. When a company's website says, "submit résumé here," and the dragnet is not collecting candidates fast enough to meet company demands for specific personnel, that's when professional recruiters are called in.

- Call the human resource departments of companies; ask human resources personnel about open opportunities and the process they recommend you follow. Let the stomach churning begin.

Does anything from the proceeding list sound familiar? For now, let us consider engaging some or all of the following:

- Put thought into the specific industry you intend to pursue. Yes! Make a decision. **Decide on your target industry! This decision is necessary and mandatory**.
- Select companies that reside within your chosen industry or area (there are many many sources to find the names of such companies, such as Hoovers, Manta, LinkedIn, Lexus-Nexus, etc.)
- Visit the websites, or collect the data using Hoovers, Manta, Facebook, LinkedIn, etc., and collect the names of two or three actual and appropriate decision makers in those companies. The company receptionist can also be called and

simply asked for the names of the decision makers. Sample decision makers' titles include: director of operations, VP finance, safety director, engineering manager, chief information officer, product development director, marketing manager, etc, etc. Actual titles will depend on the size of the company.

- Create your own pre-designed telephone pitch for the target list of decision makers. Have it in hand, rehearsed, and ready to go.
- Pick up the phone, and call these decision makers directly.
- Have an actual conversation about your value to their company, and their needs in your area of interest. Do this with as many of these decision makers as possible.
- When it makes sense, *only then send your résumé*.
- Secure yourself a job.

Ask yourself:

From which of the above lists do you prefer to put in use for your own job search, right here-and-now, at this very moment? Which is *most likely* to:

a) Vastly *increase the odds of securing a relevant job*, and

b) Vastly *increase the speed the process of securing a job*?

If the time to secure a job is shortened by even a single month, you should consider **what a month of paid employment is worth to you**. Fifteen thousand dollars per month? Three thousand dollars per month? Whatever your number, *it's not nothing*. And the savings skyrocket from there, should the process be shortened by several months, yes? Still not sure which is the best list for betting your future? Let's recap the options for performing a robust job search.

Submitting résumés thru websites, tapping personal networks, posting résumés, sending résumés to recruiters, and calling HR departments—it's time to straighten up and fly right. Decide on a target industry, select companies in that industry, collect names of decision makers from those companies, create your own custom pitch, rehearse, call the decision makers, and then speak to the decision-makers.

Take another look at the two lists above. If you selected the Second List as the best bet for your own future, please read on.

Reality Check

Does it really need to be said the goal of the job search must be reasonable in light of your abilities and experiences? That a person must be reasonably qualified for the role they seek? Let's take a minute to underscore the importance of keeping it real, because the less real you are with yourself and your expectations, the longer the odds of achieving success. For example, every day I see résumés submitted for a position as a senior oil and gas reservoir engineer from a person holding an undergraduate degree in sociology or having ten years experience as a marketing director for a real estate brokerage firm. Needless to say, there can be no reasonable expectation for this person to ever ever ever be invited for an interview for the engineering role, much less securing the reservoir engineering position. On occasion, I'll listen to impassioned speeches about how they are perfectly capable of performing well and succeeding in the role.

Who knows, maybe this assertion is true. Perhaps they could succeed and climb up a learning curve quickly, just as claimed. On and on and on with stories about how their granddad was an engineer in the oil industry, and they visited granddad quite a lot and are quite familiar with the concepts and how the engineering portion of the industry works. Again, **perhaps this is all true**. But it does not make a person a realistic candidate for the position. The question is **not** "Are you capable?" The question is *"Who is your competition?"*

In this example, the *greatest obstacle* for the applicant is the presence of all the degreed reservoir engineers having years of reservoir engineering experience with oil and gas companies! Let's leave opportunities to those who can reasonably expect to receive consideration.

You, on the other hand, *must* instead focus your efforts on real estate marketing opportunities or whatever is up your alley. Otherwise, our method will not meet the twin guarantees of securing a job faster and increasing the odds of securing that job. *In addition, your time and that of others will be wasted.* Focus on your skills and demonstrated abilities, so that you hone in quickly on realistic opportunities.

It is important to build on the value you have thus far created, value that can be promoted. A housewife, who twenty years ago worked in retail banking administration for five years, is advised against process management, but encouraged to look into any administrative position that creates a path to greater responsibility, banking or not. But, enough of that—there are reams of books to offer guidance along these lines. This guide is not one of them.

Part 2
Gaming Your Odds

Think of the value of your experiences. Take a minute to add its total value. Place the total value on a specific point of a "spectrum of value," with "incredibly marketable" on one end, and "virtually unemployable" on the other. Every single little variable (and there are perhaps dozens, hundreds, even thousands of such variables that affect each of us) accumulates and serves to move your particular value one way or another on the "spectrum of value." Now remove all rose-colored glasses. Place yourself on the "spectrum of value" even if doing so is:

- Unfair or fair
- Right or wrong
- How things should or shouldn't be
- Politically correct or politically incorrect

It's the way of the world when it comes to a job search. You must understand that most variables affecting your own marketability are simply not within your control. For another group of variables, you do have influence. The third group of great interest is the one containing variables for which you have direct control. It's this third grouping of variables on which we want to concentrate our attention, because nothing can stop a person from improving, emphasizing, enhancing, and otherwise maximizing these variables so as to move your point on the "spectrum of value" toward an overall, considerably higher value.

Maximization of some variables requires work. It's a judgment call as to how much time and effort you wish to put towards maximizing your variables. "Mark, variables? What variables? What the heck are you talking about?"

Here are a few:

- The tone and pitch of your telephone voice.
- Amount of time and effort directed at the job search.
- Level of reviewing, editing, and improving your pitch.
- Familiarizing yourself with important concepts and buzzwords common to your industry.
- Level of clarity on typical, required duties: discuss, reflect, research, consider, and re-consider the precise focus of your search in terms of job duties and responsibilities.
- Gain clarity on typical required duties.

- Firmness of your "reasonableness check"—perform a "reasonableness check" on each and every value you believe you bring to a company and the job you might fill, running past as many objective listeners as possible and accepting true critical feedback.

- How polished is your pitch? Practice your pitch in the mirror a great number of times, listening to yourself each time, adjusting toward good to better and then best.

- Level of regular exercise and a healthy diet raises confidence and places a spring in your voice. (I know, sounds like something from a "building self-esteem" book).

- How well you know who you're pitching, even if only their title.

- How many decision makers within a company you actually call.

- Quality of two stories—have in hand two stories: they should each be one minute in length, both illustrate how you have previously met a work challenge and were able to overcome and succeed due to your own skills and abilities.

In conclusion, do be prepared. Every little positive tweak of your variables games the odds further in your favor. Greater focus helps. Clarity of objectives helps.

Get Motivated, Yes!

Mark, you've got some nerve! What, you think it's OK to simply pick up the phone and start discussing career possibilities with important hiring managers? Talk about your "audacity of hope"! What about the audacity of having confidence in yourself, gaining an ability to promote self-value in a targeted way?

It's time. If you experience flutters in your stomach, sweaty palms, or anxiety, it's time to address these head-on. They serve no purpose, offer no career value, and must be summarily expunged from your system before we can press on. Mountains upon mountains of books, CDs, television series, seminars, and lectures are out there on this very topic. You must possess the ability to reach your peak confidence level, as it is critical to success in a job search, as well as in most areas of life. You need to know this if you don't already, and you need to take steps to make certain we are reaching near your peak so as to quickly reach out and grab your new career.

Mark P. Williamson

Methodology

Methodical processes work. This is especially true in engineering environments, organizational practices, and any other endeavor where you seek to increase the odds of success. I'll spare you the need for tortuous levels of differential calculus needed for an engineering degree, but the notion of applying a methodical process to achieve a favorable result is time-tested, drawing on deep experience and direct observation. And, it will work here.

No matter what the starting point, no matter how thick or thin your experiences to date, this process will vastly *increase the odds* of success in securing a job, and vastly *speed the process. As noted in the original 'advice' letter:*

DO NOT BOTHER to email, fax, or submit online your résumé through a website. (Oh yes: résumés. How to write a splendid one. Reams of books on the subject of writing a beautiful résumé exist. *This guide?* Not.)

Holy smokes! **What a colossal waste of your time!** Electronically sending a résumé to a faceless person for whom you have no connection? What do *you* think? Vastly increases or vastly decreases your odds of success? Answer: it's the worst kind of odds and has little chance of achieving your goal of securing a relevant job. Granted, it is an **easy** thing to do, does not require much thought, maybe even makes a person feel better, which is probably why the masses continue to do it. (In this hyper-electronic age, it's noteworthy that the act of publicly posting your résumé is likely to have unintended consequences, attracting spammers and empty come-ons to work from home, etc.)

For the majority of jobseekers, the electronic submission of résumés only serves to discourage a person psychologically at the precise time when he or she needs to experience uplifting activities.

How about the following alternative:

spend all your time arranging to speak to the decision makers directly, the hiring managers who decide who will fill the job openings for which you seek to capture. Once these key individuals are engaged with you in conversation, demonstrate the value you can deliver for the existing needs within their company? Just by reaching out to these people you will demonstrate skills in *communication* and *perseverance*. You tell me: *more likely* or *less likely* to affect the odds of achieving your goals vs. electronic submission of résumés to nameless, faceless people?

Regardless of your background to this point in time, you now have a goal or objective tied to your search Right? Right? Do you have a goal or objective? If not, *stop right now*, and re-visit the above advice on setting goals and objectives. You *must* know what you want! You *must* make certain that what you want passes a reasonableness test before continuing!

Part 3
The Pitch

OK. Goals and objectives should be clear in your mind, concepts you can easily articulate, but let's make sure. An example:

My goal is to secure an experienced professional position (not entry level, not supervisory level) in logistic coordination. The role can be with a logistics company *or* part of the in-house logistics department for a manufacturing company, and typically requires working knowledge of a standard logistical software package.

If prompted, you can tell a friend, in a crisp, clear, concise manner what that goal or objective is. Loudly. *Louder, speak up!* As you tell the friend the idea is to fill your voice full of:

- Confidence
- Good cheer
- Bravado

You will succeed if you are the person who can speak with emotional detachment, confident but not needy, while at the same time maintaining a diplomatic and professional speaking voice. Twists and turns aside, such a person will succeed. Whether you can become an emotionally detached diplomat is up to you and you alone.

What do I mean by professional and diplomatic? I am referring to a speaking voice, a tone, and a respect that is characterized by kindness, manners, good cheer, and clarity of purpose. You cannot be certain to whom you might speak during the course of your calls, such as receptionists and assistants; each person has their own lives, emotions, personal problems, agendas, and work pressures. You just can't be sure of the state of mind of the person on the other end of the line at the moment you call, and therefore cannot be sure how they will perceive you as you forge ahead.

What we do know, what we can be certain of, is the positive and professional attitude and tone you can deliver. This means being kind and courteous with receptionists, administrators, tech support, executives, and supervisors. It also means having clear purpose and communicating that purpose quickly and appropriately so as to not waste your time or theirs. Such an approach is refreshing and broadly appreciated in the long run, certainly over the course of all the calls you will be making.

It's important that you clearly articulate your own internal value, the value that makes you eligible and capable of reaching your goal. What might this value look like in words? **How quickly can you say these words and still be clearly understood?** What should your tone and vocal pitch sound like when you say these words? Do tone, speed, and clarity matter when it comes to maximizing your effectiveness? Yes!

This pitch or statement of both your goals and your values can include:

- Your previous relevant experiences
- Your abilities
- Your belief in yourself and why you have such conviction

You now have what is called a value statement. When a value statement is **combined** with goals, you have a pitch.

When delivering the scripted pitch to a hiring manager, the idea is to establish credibility *within ten to fifteen seconds at a time*. In other words, what is said (and how it is said) in the first ten to fifteen seconds will either convince or fail to convince the hiring manager whether he or she should continue to listen for the next ten to fifteen seconds ... yes! ten to fifteen seconds!

If the hiring manager likes the first segment of seconds, he or she just might invest in listening to the second segment of seconds. At this point credibility, intrigue, and curiosity can begin to take hold of the hiring manager as you have now become refreshing and inspiring, something the hiring manager rarely experiences. With their defenses beginning to loosen, they are relaxed and prepared to listen to the next full thirty seconds, provided that the tone, words, and speed continue to stay focused and relevant. Now is the time to stay focused, avoiding irrelevant comments and stories.

A note that we will touch upon again later is that it's **rare** to find hiring managers who will make the above investment in time and can sense impending value enough to actually listen to what you have to say. Dozens, perhaps hundreds, of pitches will need to be delivered to locate the hiring managers. Such ripe moments are found when the need for your particular talents at the target company are high, and the corresponding level of frustration with that individual in finding good and qualified candidates is also high.

Again, remember that a good number of managers already have a hiring need in their head that they have not yet shared with anyone in the company.

One take-away is: there is no need to get hung-up or attached to any particular conversation as you will have several dozen good conversations before knowing which will eventually bubble to the top as an interview or job offer. You are on an exploration to *discover* pre-existing interest. This pre-existing interest will be found residing in the heads of hiring managers, to be discovered by *you*!

You will be conducting a systematic exploration to discover the best conditions for the perfect moment to deliver a good pitch. Statistically, it is only a matter of time until success is achieved. Remember: *nothing can stop you from making such discoveries except you. You own this process.*

The opening moments of your pitch must not take more than thirty **seconds** to deliver. The overall script, although delivered in sections throughout your conversation with the decision maker, cannot take more than ninety **seconds** to deliver.

The main components of the script will include:

- A statement about who you are.
- The purpose of your call.
- Your value statement: tell her what's distinctive about you, what the particular value is that you deliver.
- Your goal or objective: tell him what exactly it is you want. Be specific, referring to job functions or job titles.
- A question: Do they have a current need for someone of your skills and abilities?

Practice and Hone Your Script

Does your pitch sound like it is being read from a page? *Not good.* If so, practice varying your voice so that you sound more conversational. Place emphasis on the most important words in each sentence, and do so naturally. Pay attention to your tone, volume, and word-emphasis. Watch your inflection! You must avoid a monotonous delivery. And be sure to smile while practicing your pitch. Believe me, people can hear you smile on the other end. Rehearse dozens of times while watching yourself in the mirror. Listen carefully and be brutally honest with yourself.

Say your script aloud a minimum of twenty times. Understand that for the great majority of us, saying a pitch with confidence and bravado does not come naturally. Practice is **essential** for developing and refining such ability. You learned to swim or ride a bike, didn't you? It took some practice, yes? **This is no different.**

Play-act the script with a friend or family member. If you cannot deliver your pitch successfully in the mirror, followed by delivery to a friend or family member, there's little or no chance the pitch can be successful with your target audience: the hiring manager. So, yes, the pitch has to go through a dry run many times until a real comfort level is achieved. Make the pitch as many times as necessary to remove the jitters and any trace of nervousness in your voice.

What's the big deal anyway? You're a person, and they're a person. No more, no less. As you will see, this practice is an investment in yourself that will pay dividends far beyond successfully securing the job you seek.

Tips for a Good Pitch

Elements of a good pitch are straightforward. They include being:

- Efficient with your words: clear in your meaning without being blabby.
- Respectful of this person's time. Ask: "Is this a good time to speak?" or "Do you have two or three minutes to speak?"
- Demonstration of insight of the company, and how that insight connects to you. "I see Mega Corp has reorganized into four geographic regions. I once was part of a team that oversaw logistics in a similar situation."
- Intelligent. Get a thesaurus. While you don't want to sound like Einstein or Shakespeare, you do want to use words in proper context that signify your intelligence and grasp of the situation. That's "signify" and not "show," see what I mean?
- Natural. Ensure your pitch sounds conversational.

Sample Pitches

Sample 1

"Hello, is this Jean Smith? This is Dan Johnson. I'm calling about logistical supervision at Mega Corp. Is now a good time to speak for two or three minutes? Great! I have a background in logistics and hold (a degree, a certification, whatever is most important or relevant to Mega Corp; an MBA in project management; a technical training certificate recognized by your industry; a certain number of hours logged such as teaching or training). I read Mega's press releases on the new operational expansion with Sigma Corp. Are you able to share how Mega will address the need for securing logistics talent, in light of current events? I'm interested in securing a role as part of these initiatives. I can only imagine how time-consuming it must be to search for the right people. What's the best way to proceed so that I can be considered?"

Sample 2

In this example, the idea is to deliver fifteen second bursts of interest to compel the listener to invest in the next fifteen second burst. Then, the listener likely begins to relax enough to invest in an entire minute or two, at which point you deliver your pitch.

"Hi, is this Jean Smith? This is Dan Johnson, is now a good time to speak for a couple of minutes? **Great!** For the last two years, I've been running a product development firm that has a distribution network throughout the US Southeast, but I'm now selling it to secure a more stable role." (There is your first fifteen seconds, so make it **compelling**.) "I am aware that Mega Corp develops similar products, but on a much larger scale, of course—very impressive. May I ask how growth has been coming along in this economic climate, generally speaking? Cool. (Say something here that builds on the answer she just provided by indicating you have a shared experience. This is your *second* fifteen-second burst; now she's ready to listen for a good two minutes.)

"My business has been focused on home accessories targeted towards children and 'kidults' and upmarket luxury design targeted towards lovers of contemporary art and design. Our most notable product achieved sales of six million dollars (or whatever the accurate number is)."

(Now be quiet; see how she replies, step back, get a "read" as to how the conversation is going, and adapt. Keep it simple! Is the reaction enthusiastic? Is it uncomfortable? Is it lukewarm? If it's either of the latter descriptions, it means you've not yet convinced her she has an interest in what you're saying.

If Enthusiastic:

Engage in a robust conversation, but MAKE SURE the conversation remains balanced, right near 50/50 (you speak 50 percent, they speak 50 percent). Of course, it is easier to control how much you say, as in you can choose to speak more or less. The real challenge of keeping a conversation balanced arises when the other person attempts to dominate the conversation by attempting to do all the talking. Remember, you can gather strength from the philosophy that you don't care that much or are simply confident in the importance of your own message. Therefore, you are prepared to assert yourself and stop the hiring manager's blabbing. An effective way to do this (while remaining professional and diplomatic) is to simply, yet firmly say, "Hang on, hang on, hang on," until they stop talking, then say with a spirited chuckle "We'll get to all that..." and continue with your next point.

Sound too tough? Take further comfort that you have nothing to lose. If the person will not stop talking or becomes offended by your tactics, then you have discovered at a very early stage *a career involving this person will never work out.* You just saved a heap of time and trouble.

On the other hand, if they take the cue and let you speak, it's a sign from them of respect and professional courtesy, thus a path that continues to show promise.

Luke-warm

Ask more non-invasive questions about her and offer more details about your efforts that drove the two years and six million dollars in sales. Keep going until you sense an improving level of interest.

Uncomfortable

Ask them about their current initiatives. What sort of challenges are currently blocking or slowing progress toward the execution of those initiatives? Keep asking intelligent questions; gather as much general information about them and the industry as possible.

Notice you have still not yet mentioned your interest in working with them; but so far in the process you *have* created some traction or connectedness with this person. She is now somewhat vested in the conversation. Now you can lower the boom. Ask questions about their need for people in your area of interest or expertise and express an interest in working with them in some capacity, steer the conversation in this direction.

By the way, let's not lose sight that, apart from your investment in this guide (thank you), all of this preparation and effort is free of charge. The preparation costs you nothing. During the period that a person is unemployed, *time* is a plentiful resource; money is a resource that's harder to come by, but that one seeks to secure. For the vast majority, the path to cash and a livelihood is greatly shortened via this process than all other traditional job-seeking methods. I say majority, because there will always be unknown variables that may work for or against a person, such as luck, the off-chance when traditional job seeking methods work, or that friend/family connections comes through.

Part 4

The Call List

Shall We Dance?

You have your pitch ready. You have reached a confident level of comfort in delivering your pitch. Who exactly are you going to call? We now need a target audience to receive your pitch. The second half of your quest to ***increase odds of success and speed favorable results*** comes in the form of the creation of a list of hiring managers. Yes, their names, phone numbers, and titles will be needed.

Lucky for us, we live in an age of incredible resources, an ability to gather all the information you need from the Internet (or Internet supplemented by a few calls). Having defined your goals and objectives, and having run a good "reasonableness test," certain industries will be implied due to their proximity to where you reside.

Consider various approaches:

- Google lists of companies within industries
- Social networking sites such as LinkedIn and Facebook are outstanding for this purpose

- Visit free company search sites mentioned earlier, such as Manta, which are designed for such a search
- Other "pay-for" services, such as Hoover or Lexis-Nexis, can be accessed at a local library
- Read industry directories (such as Thompsons). Some are accessible via the Internet, others are on reserve at your local library
- Try also *Reference USA*, a free online search database of US businesses

Once you have the names of companies, finding the names of potential hiring managers is fairly easy via LinkedIn. Type in the company name, watch the names of current employees come back.

Seek to pile up **at least** 100 companies in your industries. Two or three hundred companies are even better. **Do the work.** Search and pile, search and pile, search and pile target names. Create your list. For each company, you need to gather the names and titles of as many decision makers as possible. These names and titles might be online (but only sometimes) or in directories. If you are unable to drum up at least two names per company (three to five names per company is preferable) online, then give the main number a call and ask for the names that hold the management titles you seek.

Yes, creating this list will take some time, probably a number of days. *It's important to create the list all at once before moving forward in the process.* That's OK. In fact, in the process of simply creating the list, you will acquire significant knowledge of the industry you are targeting, meaning by necessity and definition you will become more knowledgeable of the target industry than *other candidates with whom you are competing for the job openings*!

More knowledgeable = increased odds of securing the job, a nice variable to have in your pocket.

By the end of your search for target companies and target hiring manager names and titles, your calling list should add up to somewhere between 200 (100 companies, two names per company) to 600 names (200 companies, three names per company). Create an Excel spreadsheet, or simply write on paper a list in five columns:

- Name of hiring manager
- Name of company
- Telephone of hiring manager (most times, this will be the main number)
- Title of hiring manager
- Notes

Manage the Process

Getting organized, managing your time, staying on point, staying focused on the task at hand, staying true to your selected area of job focus, and your own organizational skills - each make for good sound bites. Sounds great. Most people assume they have these skills, maybe so.

Putting together your call list is *hard work*. It takes long hours of concentration and commitment. Becoming distracted is all too easy. We all have busy lives and have many people, places, and things that catch our eye. That's obvious.

What is not so obvious is: *the human tendency towards procrastination when confronted with hard work or having to think.* Creating your call list, creating your pitch, deciding on your best values all require high levels of brainpower. With such a huge cerebral undertaking ahead, it becomes easy and tempting to rationalize and convince yourself that, at any particular moment, something more important needs to be attended to. Don't get caught in a trap that you'll get back to your research of companies and hiring managers, such as:

- Reading up on developments in related industries.
- Reading up on what the federal government has to say about regulations and legislation in your selected industry.

- Reading emails that have just arrived from Mom containing career ideas to explore. (*Maybe I should give Mom a call.*)
- Wow! What a cool new app!
- "Oh look! There is my 1983 copy of *What Color Is My Parachute?* (*Maybe I should give it a good re-reading.*)
- I really should clip my toenails.
- Etc.

To avoid such back-sliding and diversions that will only serve to drag out this process and allow a sense of "this isn't working" to creep into your head, set daily actionable, measurable goals and let nothing prevent the attainment of the daily goal. If it's decided that 200 names of hiring managers is achievable and reasonable, perhaps a good daily goal is the gathering of twenty names (and performing the research necessary to find those names).

In this way, you experience daily success as you march toward the Big Day: the day cold calling begins.

Making the Calls

Dun, dun, DUNNNNNNNNNNNNNN... Now, you are ready to call. Nervousness, although a reaction quite natural for calling people you don't know, greatly decreases the odds of success. Self-confidence sells.

So, if you're overwhelmed with nervousness, it's time to circle back to practicing your pitch in the mirror to friends and family. Can't do it in front of a mirror or circle of friends and family? Then you're not ready for primetime. You need to feel confident before you call.

Here's a thought to ponder. The person on the other end of the line of any of these calls (including the calls placed to gather names of hiring managers, and calls placed directly to the hiring managers) is just that, a person. You're a person. They're a person. At the end of the day, they are no better or worse than you. *In the blink of an eye, the person you are calling may themselves soon be reading this guide and applying its techniques.* We are all one breath from humility. Keep this in mind and keep cool. You're calling another human being, so what? What's the Big Deal? There is none!

OK. Now, with your call list in place and confidence at a sufficient level to make effective calls, let's call.

Make calls to each and every decision maker. The best way to do this is in sections of twenty names. Divide the names into groups of twenty. For each group of names, dial each person, one right after the other, until all names are called. Expect dialing to take forty to seventy-five minutes to complete. Be sure and take a fifteen-minute break afterwards.

Do not let anything stop you from calling all twenty names! If you need ice breaking to get started, make the first group of twenty names you care the least about.

Now:

- Unplug/turn off other phones.
- Turn off all other distractions.
- Do not engage in any other activity until the entire group of twenty names has been dialed.

Do not worry about the outcome of each call. By this, I mean a call can result in a number of possible outcomes, including:

- A wrong number
- A voicemail
- A secretary or receptionist
- The wrong person
- The hiring manager herself

If a wrong number:

Note this in the "notes" column of your spreadsheet. Do not make corrections until you have completed calling ALL 20 NAMES ! ! !

If the wrong person:

Ask them for the correct number of your target person and note on your spreadsheet.

When it comes to voicemail:

Here's an opportunity to deliver your entire one-minute pitch without interruption. You can expect voicemail to represent the lion's share of outcomes for dialing the first time. So, it takes a little preparation and readiness to deliver. All of your mirror preparation will come in quite handy, the caveat being the pitch must be very close to one-minute in length. All the points must be included, so a brisk, clear pace needs to be maintained to get through it all without being too speedy. And, you have to leave a return phone number.

If a secretary, receptionist, or assistant to the hiring manager:

This requires a little nimbleness of both thought and mouth. Remember, you do have the ability to control what *you* do and say. You cannot control what others will do or say, so *don't worry about it*. A secretary or receptionist, not knowing anything about you or your intentions, can often become abrasive. Just doing his job, right? In such a case, in order to maintain higher odds of success, don't worry about the person's reaction. Some calls will work out according to plan, but *many will not*.

Good, bad, or ugly:

remember there is always another hiring manager to be called.

In any event, you may be asked the purpose of your call, or something to that affect.

Here are a few solid possible responses:

- "I'm calling regarding an employment opportunity in (insert the hiring manager's department here)."
- "I'm calling regarding a business discussion relating to (insert the hiring manager's department here)."
- "It's a confidential matter about (insert the name of the hiring manager's area here)."
- "I'm calling regarding a business opportunity in (insert the hiring manager's department here)."

In all cases, no matter what the reaction or tone of the secretary or receptionist, remain cheerful and polite. Do not . . . DO **NOT** get:

- Mad
- Abrasive
- Sarcastic

- Irked
- Irritated

With this person, no matter how:

- Rude ("Don't bother us!")
- Petty ("We don't accept outside calls.")
- Nosey ("Who is this?")
- Mean ("Good luck, ha ha ha"), or
- Curt ("Don't callback.")

they are with you.

Instead, kill them with kindness and perfect manners. Say, "Thank you for your time and assistance!" in your most positive, natural tone. If ever there were a time to *NOT* burn a bridge, this is it. Leave a benign impression, you will be remembered. Benign keeps your odds riding high. Make a note of exactly what was said, the name of the secretary or receptionist, and then move on to the next call.

If the hiring manager answers, it's "go" time. Have your spreadsheet ready.

Should you actually get a target decision maker on the phone, and the person is able and willing to hear your pitch, you will at that moment have launched yourself into an opportunistic interview. You should be prepared and ready to make things happen. Recall that we want the first fifteen seconds of what we say to convince the person to invest in the next fifteen seconds, right?

Back to the first fifteen seconds:

Offer an appropriate greeting (favorites include "hello," "good morning," and "good afternoon"). Confirm whom you are speaking with: "Is this Mr. Johansson? Great!"

Then, introduce yourself. with "My name is…"

Next, say something like "I'm a logistics coordinator with strong logistics skills, and I am calling to speak with you about a career opportunity." So far, so good.

If during these fifteen seconds, you came across someone who is upbeat, polite, and professional, it's refreshing, so go for it. The person is likely to invest in listening to you for another fifteen seconds.

"Is now a good time for you, do you have a couple of minutes? Great!

From what I understand, Mega Corp has an ongoing need for people experienced in logistics coordination, management, possibly even logistics design. Is that generally right?"

OK, so far so good. The person is right on the edge of engaging you in a conversation.

"I have experience with precisely these types of activities and want to get a clearer picture of Mega's current needs in its logistical operations." If the person is still engaged in the conversation at this point, you have entered the zone in which you want to be to have an honest and candid conversation about what their company needs and how your experiences and abilities can be valuable.

If you confirm they're looking for what you offer, some follow-up questions to ask include:

"That's great to hear. What range of experience are you looking for? Both entry-level and senior level? I myself have seven years of experience, some of it supervisory, plus experience with the logistics software (while you need to brief, be specific whenever possible with your answers)." Your goal at this point is to split the time asking a good number of relevant, intelligent questions, but also offering further relevant details about your own experiences and abilities. Balance the conversation. It works. It is respectful of time. It exhibits professional behavior.

Be sure to work questions into the conversation naturally, do not just read the following list rapid-fire. Sounds aggressive, unprofessional, and disrespectful. It's OK if everything is not covered in this first conversation. Remember, if all goes well, other conversations will follow with more opportunities to get all points on the table. Samples:

- How many logistics professionals is Mega looking to hire?

- What is the timeframe of the hiring process? When is Mega looking to have people in place?
- What events at Mega have created the current hiring need?
- Where will these roles office?

Avoid boneheaded questions, such as questions for which the answer appears on Mega's homepage.

Mega will want to know reasons you're pursuing Mega for a job. The answer is not "Because I need a job." Instead, how about: "I enjoy logistics and am looking for an opportunity that will allow me to leverage my experience." Or, "My solid experience in logistics and in the use of malware, which I've supervised informally will help me step into a formal supervisory role."

In any event, keep things moving along. Be aware of how much time is passing (do be respectful of their time!), and steer the conversation to a close with a statement like "Mr. Johansson, it's been a pleasure, thank you for taking the time. Oh, before I forget, what's your best email address? I'll send you an updated version of my résumé, then let's set a time to speak further and move forward."

At this point, it's not a good idea to be presumptuous and refer to an upcoming meeting. Let Mr. Johansson make such a suggestion, if he wants to.

The game is to speak to so many Johanssons, that enough of them will actually take steps to pursue you and to arrange for an interview.

That's why it is so important to keep going until you have spoken with 75 percent of your call list. Also, it's difficult to articulate the value of *momentum*. Don't pause/stop/take a break to ponder, *just keep calling!* Forward motion builds confidence and yields better results—pausing does not. If that's not convincing enough, how about this: you will suffer less by calling without stopping and without thinking about it between calls.

One cannot be sure how the breaks are going to go with these calls:

- People think things over and change their minds, both to the positive and to the negative.
- People get distracted and don't get back to you in the timeframe mentioned, *even though they intended to.*
- *Situations change* in companies, suddenly rendering statements made by Johansson to be irrelevant and invalid, through no fault of Johansson.

Many times, the breaks will go your way, but you must work to increase the odds by calling and speaking with more hiring managers. Like my dad always said, "You're not going to catch a fish without a hook in the water."

So, keep going. Don't rest on your laurels. *Laurel resting is for those not reading this guide.*

After your first hour of twenty calls, *record in great detail who you spoke to, what exactly was said by both you and the decision maker. Include*:

- Titles
- Departments
- Phone numbers
- Email
- Who they report to
- What they mentioned doing last weekend
- What's currently causing them frustration

Virtually any information can be used later to your positive advantage.

So take the time to write good notes, if at all possible, as you're speaking. At the very least, make notes immediately upon conclusion of the conversation. It is the insights flowing from these notes that will be leveraged in subsequent calls! Being able to refer to real details in future calls creates credibility and traction; it also **motivates** the parties to action toward *your* objectives, makes your agenda appear worth their time and effort!

So, include observations and noteworthy reactions about the hiring manager. Anything that can possibly offer insight as to the value of further conversation with this person must be noted. Later, you will guard your time and further increase the odds of success by deciding which hiring managers merit further discussion. So all indicators as to their interest in you, openness as to their existing needs, and willingness to discuss with you should be carefully noted.

Exciting. An indication of interest. Doesn't that feel better than rotting while you wait for a response to an online résumé submission? And isn't that a bit more uplifting to your spirits, further boosting your attitude and making subsequent calls that much better?

However, do not stop calling simply because you have early success! Be sure to call your entire list, no matter what! One cannot be certain what will come of any of these promising conversations, so it is imperative to keep going until you have an attractive written offer for employment in your hand.

For those hiring managers not reached the first time, call a second, third, even fourth time (call them, but *don't leave multiple messages*; that might make you sound needy).

Keep calling until you have had a conversation with at least 75 percent of every decision maker on your call list.

Leave a second voicemail message once a few days have passed since leaving the initial voicemail message. Don't leave a third voice message no matter how much time passes.

If helpful, consider an "icon" system to help quickly identify the call status for each hiring manager:

:)   to indicate interest

*   to indicate you left a voice message

X   to indicate a wrong number, and

: (to indicate he/she is just not interested

Why Not the HR Department: The Case Against

I can make a compelling case as to why an HR department is not the place to begin your job search. Often, calls will result in your being transferred immediately to the human resources department of your target firm. On the surface, this makes sense. Aren't they the department that helps folks such as you locate and secure a job?

In all fairness, that is but one of several job functions performed by HR. Much of their time is occupied by:

- Issues relating to current employees
- The administration of benefits
- 401Ks
- Health insurance
- Legal issues
- Issues relating to company morale
- Corporate communication and policy

The time allotted to find and hire new employees is limited. And this time allotment is often characterized by the administration of writing and placing advertisements, maintaining job descriptions and listings on the company website and elsewhere, and sifting through thousands and thousands of résumés that are mailed, emailed, and downloaded from the website. When thousands of pieces of paper are viewed day after day after day, *it becomes mind numbing and difficult to decipher who is interview-worthy and who is not.* Additionally, they must be responsive to ever-increasing needs of internal hiring managers. Believe me when I say they are unwilling to invest random, unscheduled bits of time on a person that simply calls them, **no way!**

Yes, it never ends in the HR department. Many times, a thankless job if ever there was a thankless job.

How the hell can you distinguish yourself or otherwise grab HR's attention in such adverse circumstances? You can't. It is an unforgiving and inexact process that will never play up to your strengths.

Getting HR on the phone is not much better. You can be the greatest salesperson who ever lived, have an amazing telephone voice with the most polished pitch ever, yet your words are likely to fall on deaf ears in the HR department. HR can hardly hear you over the roar of rustling résumés sitting in front of them at that very moment. They will likely offer directions to their website or a postal address to submit a résumé. It's the way of the world, accept it and move on to a plan that has some chance of success.

In conclusion, *DO NOT SPEAK WITH HR!* It's better to move on to the next company than engage with any person in HR. So, include a strategy to stay focused on your goal of speaking directly to the decision maker. The typical question asked, "*May I ask what is this in regards to?*" means you need to have ready an answer designed to get you to the decision maker. Examples:

- "I am following up to a previous call (say this only if true)."
- "In regards to a discussion regarding Mega's environmental cleanup efforts in Southeast Asia (provided they do indeed have such an issue)."
- "I have a consulting question regarding business development strategies outlined in (the decision maker's) division."
- "I am preparing a presentation for (the hiring manager's) department, but need to touch base with her."

In any case, close off paths that lead to HR:

- Obtain the best information you can get on the direct lines of hiring managers.
- Try calling another department within the target company and ask to be transferred to the decision maker.
- Try working your way through the telephone employee search options when given the chance.

75 percent: First Down and Goal to Go

Remember: keep calling until you achieve the very measurable goal of speaking directly to at a minimum 75 percent of your call list. That was the hard part. Now, it is necessary to create many follow-up conversations with both the decision maker and others in the company, with whom the decision maker may want you to speak. *Now you see why the need for superior and precise note taking of previous conversations.*

The perception of your own credibility is significantly connected to your ability to incorporate and refer to important information, *specific information from previous conversations*, as well as correct usage of the names of those with whom you have already spoken. Especially valuable are *insights* into the company, recent changes in the company, and the importance of the position you seek. These insights are a giant step toward becoming a perceived insider: a person who is smart and well informed about things that matter to the person with whom they are speaking, the company itself, and the company's needs for a qualified person.

As you work in insightful information gathered from previous conversations, simultaneously express your own value in such a way that *the insight and value become connected*. For example, if the hiring manager previously mentioned Mega's upcoming need to hire five logistics analysts who have worked with freight forwarding companies, you can say, "When I was with Alpha Corporation, I worked on a six-month project for the Hyundai freight forwarding account, installing new software and trouble-shooting their system and removing all bugs." Or, "Last time we spoke, you mentioned a concern that the marketing analysts you hired will need familiarity with acquisitions issues, due to Mega Corp's upcoming merger with Alpha Corp. When I was with Omega Corp in 2009, I was the content coordinator for all press releases, checking facts, yes, but also enhancing content."

In doing so, multiple job opportunities are likely to emerge, opportunities that may not yet exist on the website, but *only exist in the minds of decision makers as a pestering need*—and here you are in a conversation that could save the decision maker mountains of time and effort, since they have someone as industrious and impressive as you on the phone!

When such a scenario arises, you have created your own opportunity and why not? It's a natural offshoot of making calls to decision makers and demonstrating industriousness, insight, and value! *Why not you?*

You have now placed yourself at the door of the traditional interview process, with one supreme exception: *You've already had conversations with the decision makers of your target company, someone who you have undoubtedly impressed with your initiative and resolve.* The decision maker is glad to have facilitated bringing onboard such a person.

Furthermore, you will have harvested an incredible collection of insights for which the hiring company will likely place a value.

Independently, when the process is over and you have been hired (What did I tell you? *Much faster—more like what you had in mind!*), you'll also have created an outstanding Rolodex of decision makers in your industry! Some of these decision makers, now that they know who you are and what you are capable of, just might have a future interest in you too!

Part 5
You Be the Judge

Notes on Conventional Sources of Help

As mentioned, there are several well-known conventional sources of job-seeking assistance. There is not one doubt each of them can and do actually work to some degree. People find jobs through conventional sources, hope I have not mislead otherwise.

At issue is the speed and accuracy of the results of these methods. I will strongly argue that, by comparison to the approach suggested in this guide, all conventional methods are woefully slow, often inaccurate, and are far *less likely* to secure the job you actually **want.**

Government

The government is managing statistics, offering sound bites, and trying to get its members re-elected. There's lots of grandstanding and bravado, as well as enormous rhetoric and open concern about creating jobs, decreasing unemployment, endless talk on this subject. So ask yourself: on a personal level, a level that will affect you specifically and directly and in a timely manner, where, oh where, will state or federal government take actions to either increase the odds of you securing a job or increase the speed required to secure a job?

Government is not motivated by the affects to the bottom line from staffing success or failure. It is not a for-profit entity, so be sure to set your expectations accordingly.

Recruiters

Recruiters are in search of specific individuals desired by client companies. Understand that recruiters or "head-hunters" operate as follows:

- They build a collection of clients (companies) that are in need of professional help in finding qualified and talented people, especially those that tend to be difficult to find.

- Through various means, recruiters then set off to find these talented and qualified people.

- When recruiters find the *specific* individuals sought by their clients companies, and verify the individuals are qualified and talented as defined by the client company, recruiters then collect a fee from the company. Let's be clear: *recruiters don't collect a fee from the individuals, and therefore, recruiters don't work on behalf of individuals.*

The bottom line here is: recruiters will not and cannot help you find a job, unless you happen to be one of the two or three dozen people sought by the recruiter on behalf of their client. They cannot or will not help you, because it does not pay them to help you. They are not organized to help you. Time to look elsewhere for help in your job search.

Personal Network

Friends and family networks quickly run dry; pressing forward is a helluva lot of work. Your job search is both specific and personal. All of your friends and family members each have their own lives, challenges, commitments, and responsibilities. The extent of their ability to help in a meaningful way is limited. Sure, they will make a couple of calls or even make a quick effort to contact someone who may have information or insight to help you. The odds of anyone within this network conjuring up a true path or connection that is specific to your needs, timely, and results in the successful securing of a meaningful role in your target industry is quite low. I'm not saying it *never* happens; I'm saying it's a low-odds proposition. There must be a better solution.

Job Boards

How do job boards operate? How do the job board companies (Monster, Career Builder, etc.) make their money? Job board companies make money in two primary ways: 1) companies pay job board firms a fee to post job listings online, and 2) job board companies also sell advertising space. So whom do the job board companies cater to? Like recruiters, job board companies cater to the very specific needs of client companies, as opposed to catering to the needs of the individuals seeking a job. That's right: job boards are not designed to address your specific job search challenges any better than the other so-called sources of help!

Better keep looking for a better way.

College Placement Office

The placement office at school can provide decent information, but how will they help to specifically distinguish or promote you? At first glance, it seems a bit more promising, doesn't it? After all, we are talking about your own college or university! Wasn't the placement office specifically established to help you get a job? Did the school spend a lot of money building the office space, installing an army of computers, and hire a group of career-specialist professionals to help you get a job?

You (or your mom, dad, or grandparents) just paid somewhere in the neighborhood of $30,000 to $240,000 for you to attend your school and secure a degree, which was hard enough! Why then can't the school get you a job? What the hell have they been doing with all that money, if not anticipating and preparing for the day you would graduate and need a job?

Placement offices surely deliver value—make no mistake about it. But they, too, are catering to the companies who make (sometimes large) donations to your fair school. And the wants and needs of the companies get primary attention, not the specifics of your personal job search. Placement office personnel themselves get evaluated in part by the number of students who actually secure a job. Sounds good for you, right? Yes, except that the placement office is also playing the odds, matching individuals with the opportunities *most likely* to work out. For all else, they offer resources: advice, books (there are reams of them), company information, internal job boards, access to research, etc. And by the way, if you have access to such research, definitely can be value-added when used in combination with this guide, but in the end, it's completely up to you whether you actually secure a job. If the resources of the placement office do not yield speedy results, all you will receive from them is continued sympathy and emotional support. Try paying the rent with that.

Surely, These Folks Can Help?

Did you know companies exist having the sole purpose of locating open jobs, then getting you hired? *"Holy Smokes, that sure sounds promising! Mark, why did you not speak up until now?"*

Here's why: even such companies hired to perform a job search on your behalf, I'm talking about a company for which you have paid your own money to help, have several downsides:

1) Ultimately they offer no guarantee of actually getting you a job (!).

2) They have a built-in conflict of interest: the moment you actually do secure a job, they lose all chance of extracting more fees from you.

3) Typical fees range from $3,500 to $10,000.

4) While you will receive a litany of assurances and pep talks, they are not in the same hurry you are.

5) No one, but no one can sit inside your head and perform on your behalf even a quarter as good as having you in the driver's seat. And since circumstances are always changing, and rulings must be made as situations unfold, such firms become a layer of administration wedged between your brain and the target organizations and hiring authorities. Not good for you.

And let's see how they perform in a down economy! Good luck with that.

What's Missing?

As you can see, no other source of so-called career assistance can really make much of a stride in helping you specifically. All of the above makes a few assumptions about your marketability, talent, experience, age, and personal situation. All are lacking in delivering the *passion* about yourself and your capabilities that *only you can* deliver.

But beyond this limitation, what if your own situation renders these same assumptions invalid? As mentioned previously:

- Suppose you have had special circumstances affect your marketability.
- Suppose you have no experience in the field you wish to enter.
- Suppose you were a stay-at-home mom and now wish to re-enter the workforce for the first time in twenty years.
- Suppose you encountered a string of bad luck.
- Suppose you really have had a problem getting along with co-workers and, though you have truly learned from tragic mistakes in the workplace, are now finding it hard to shake the stigma of your work history.

- Or, perhaps up until now you have only taken part-time or short-term (contract) work, but have now reached a point wherein all the benefits of a fulltime gig are what you seek?

Try to even imagine the above list of organizations helping overcome the above sampling of circumstances, when that same list is often of little value even under the best circumstances? Now what?

You still need and want a good job.

Conclusions

A job search is one of the most energy-draining, intense efforts ever made by an individual. Nothing could be more personal, more you-centric than a job search. Unless one beats long odds and gets really lucky, or happens to be exceptionally gifted (in which case: why are you even involved in a job search?), this recruiter argues that conventional job-search methods are all significantly flawed. These flaws might not be such a big deal if job search results were not so intensely important and urgent.

Eventually, most people will get a job. But, does a person care whether that job comes in one month or six months? *YES! Obviously.*

Does a person care whether he or she lands a job working the drive-thru window at a fast-food joint or analyzing investment alternatives in the corporate finance department? *YES! Definitely.*

The method described herein provides a way around long delays in securing employment or the pressure to accept less. It removes control from those people and institutions that have much less of a vested interest in the outcome and places primary control of your search directly into your own hands. Successful application of the method, a dedicated effort, and guarantees to increase the odds of securing the type of job sought and vastly reduces the time needed to secure it.

Best wishes, and happy hunting.

www.ingramcontent.com/pod-product-compliance
Lightning Source LLC
Chambersburg PA
CBHW022126170526
45157CB00004B/1775